W9-AHG-749

DAD RULES

TREION MULLER

DAD RULES

A SIMPLE MANUAL FOR A COMPLEX JOB

TREION MULLER

Plain Sight Publishing
An Imprint of Cedar Fort, Inc.
Springville, Utah

© 2012 Treion Muller
All rights reserved.

No part of this book may be reproduced in any form whatsoever, whether
by graphic, visual, electronic, film, microfilm, tape recording, or any other
means, without prior written permission of the publisher, except in the case
of brief passages embodied in critical reviews and articles.

ISBN 13: 978-1-4621-1031-5

Published by Plain Sight Publishing, an imprint of Cedar Fort, Inc.
2373 W. 700 S., Springville, UT 84663
Distributed by Cedar Fort, Inc., www.cedarfort.com

LIBRARY OF CONGRESS CATALOGING-IN-PUBLICATION DATA

Muller, Treion, 1972- author.
Dad rules : a simple manual for a complex job / Treion Muller.
pages cm
Summary: A quick go-to guide of essential rules to help fathers know what
   to expect, what to say, and what to do in difficult moments.
ISBN 978-1-4621-1031-5
1. Child rearing--Handbooks, manuals, etc. 2. Fathers--Handbooks,
   manuals, etc. 3. Father and child. 4. Fatherhood. I. Title.

HQ772.M69 2012
306.874'2--dc23

                                    2012001011

Cover design by Brian Halley
Cover design © 2012 by Lyle Mortimer
Edited and typeset by Michelle Stoll

Printed in the United States of America

10 9 8 7 6 5 4 3 2 1

Printed on acid-free paper

In loving memory of
Lily Ann

Dedicated to
Chloe, Layla, Ruby,
Gemma, and TJ

Praise for
Dad Rules

"Treion Muller provides a realistic, convincing, and witty perspective to the challenges and celebrations of fatherhood. *Dad Rules* is a must-read for all dads."

—Sean Covey, author,
The 7 Habits of Highly Effective Teens

"Fatherhood is the most important role a man can fill, and yet there aren't many classes or lessons on how to be a good father. *Dad Rules* is a humorous yet thoughtful guide to help fathers become the men they need to become for their children."

—Richard Paul Evans, #1 New York Times
bestselling author, *The Christmas Box*

"We have thought for years . . . that what this world needs is more good books for fathers. Fathership is not easy in this world, and dads need help. That is exactly what Treion Muller gives us, and he does it in the straightforward, no-nonsense, bottom-line way that men can appreciate. His 81 rules will not only help you be a better father, they will make you more glad that you are one!"

—Richard and Linda Eyre, authors,
New York Times #1 bestseller *Teaching Your Children Values,*
and founders of valuesparenting.com

"There is so much good we can do in the world, and it all starts in the home. Being a good dad has never been more important. *Dad Rules* is an engaging book that will help dads make a difference where it matters most.

—Stephen R. Covey, bestselling author,
The 7 Habits of Highly Effective People and *The 3rd Alternative*

"These thought-provoking rules helped me change and be a better father. Every father should read this unique, enjoyable book."

—Sam Bracken, author, *My Orange Duffel Bag:
A Journey to Radical Change*

Contents

Introduction

S ome dads are brand new. Some dads have a few years of fatherhood experience under their belt. Some dads have survived the infamous teenage years, and there are some who can proudly add "grand" to their title.

Regardless of where you fall on the fatherhood continuum, being a dad can be hard. There is no manual of instructions or fairy godfather to show the way. No voice from heaven or crystal ball to warn of impending danger. To add to this already complex conundrum, each child is different. What works for one may not work for another (and in most cases doesn't).

Despite these seemingly impossible odds, there are a few basic rules that, if followed, can make the journey much more enjoyable. In *Dad Rules,* you will find a collection of these rules focused on helping fathers understand what they should know, say, and do—because let's be honest, there are plenty of awkward moments when you just don't have the foggiest idea of what you should say or do.

There will be some rules that you have already mastered, some that no longer apply, and some that you won't like. There may even be rules you choose to ignore, or that you disagree with, but when you find yourself in another tricky situation you'll be grateful you have these rules to come back to.

All 81 rules in the book represent years of experiences, study, and mistakes—some from personal experience, some from observing other dads, some from the review of books and articles, and some from actually asking other patriarchs how on earth they did it. In other words, this manual is the combined wisdom of many dads who have faced similar challenges and survived.

Trust me, I am *not* an expert at being a father. On the contrary, I still have a very long way to go before my children nominate me for father of the year. No, my band of brothers, I have written this manual as much for me as for you. However, I am pretty good at recognizing good parenting when I see it, and I am consciously working on being a better father every day. (In other words, I am trying to follow Rule 1.)

How you read *Dad Rules* is up to you. While the rules are grouped into three sections, they are not in any specific order. Don't think you have to read it cover to cover. It is a manual, after all. Go to the sections or rules that interest you. Skip over the rules that you feel do not apply (yet) or that you have already mastered. But most of all, as you go over the rules, try to evaluate what type of dad you are and what type of dad you want to be, and then put on your "World's Best Dad" hat and get to work.

> *"Happiness is when what you think, what you say, and what you do are in harmony. Always aim at complete harmony of thought and word and deed. Always aim at purifying your thoughts and everything will be well."*
>
> —*Gandhi*

PART 1:

What Dads
Should Know

Part 1:

What Dads Should Know

T he rules in this section can also be called the "just deal with it" rules, because in many instances that's exactly what you have to do. You may not want to hear this, but being a good father may literally require blood, sweat, and years.

This section of the book is intended to help you with the unknown and the unexpected things that you need to—but probably don't—know.

Rule 1:
Show up for the job every day.

If you want to be a great dad, then you cannot put in a part-time effort. There are as many different kinds of dads in the world as there are dads, ranging from the absentee dad to the super-involved dad. What type of dad will you be?

Choose carefully, because the choice you make will not only determine your behavior and your child's future behavior, but it will also lead to a completely different set of consequences.

Think about it. Is your boss, your bowling buddy, or your personal trainer going to change your diapers when you are old enough to need them? Not a chance. But your children may . . . if you were around to change theirs.

"To be in your children's memories tomorrow, you have to be in their lives today."

—*Anonymous*

Rule 2:
Driving a minivan
is inevitable.

There is no room for egos or sports cars when you have children. Yes, be prepared to give up your man card. Just ask all of the former "jocks" who have traded in their Corvettes for Caravans.

(In case you were wondering, Suburbans and Escalades also apply to this rule.)

Rule 3:
Throw-up and toxic diapers come with the job.

"Cowboy up" and help your wife with these smelly tasks. By the way, you are on your own with this one, brother. Don't bother calling in a favor from your best friend, favorite uncle, or flag football teammate, because I can guarantee you will be flying solo on this rule. Just remember that soap and water were meant for times like these, and no man has died from changing a diaper . . . yet. Good luck.

Daddy Data: In case you were wondering, it is estimated that each child will need to be changed 6,000 times in the first two years of life[1]—a cost of at least $1,600.[2] To learn everything you need to know about diapers, baby rashes, and baby poop, check out babycenter.com.

Rule 4:
Ask other dads for directions.

Y ou can't possibly know everything. It's completely acceptable to seek advice from other dads, especially your own. I know that it is generally believed that men are genetically unable of asking for directions or seeking advice from someone else. I am here to tell you that this stereotype is incorrect.

Try it. I know there are other dads you admire and respect. If they have been through what you are going through, I can promise they will be more than happy to help you "fix" your problem. Make sure you remind them to also share the things they did that didn't work. I am living proof that this rule works and doesn't cause spontaneous human combustion.

Rule 5:
Refrain from trying to fix everything, especially your children's feelings.

Speaking of fixing things (see Rule 4), if you want to fix something, work on appliances or remodeling. Appliances and construction work come with a set of instructions; children don't. (Disclaimer: This manual is a set of rules for you, not a set of instructions for your children.)

However, this rule doesn't mean you shouldn't try to fix the things you can fix. There are times when a hug or a few kind words will do the trick rather well, and there are times when more action and involvement is required. So be wise enough to know when to put on your emotional utility belt and when to put it away.

Rule 6:
Babies don't sleep the whole night through, and neither should you.

Fulfill your part of the deal; this child is partly your doing. I tried using the excuse that I have to get up and go to work. I was quickly introduced to the weekend shift.

And for those of you whose wife works too, you will just have to take your turn in the rocking chair, my brother.

Daddy Data: While each baby is a little different, they do initially sleep in short bouts—typically ranging from thirty minutes to four hours—at seemingly random times throughout the day and night.[3]

Rule 7:
Your yard, car, electronic devices, and favorite recliner will be trashed.

Toys, clothes, and "sticky stuff" will appear from nowhere to clutter up your life. You may have a spotless house one minute and a mess the next. But, thankfully, melted candy bars do come off car seats, and gum can be removed from the La-Z-Boy with a little effort and, yes, the aforementioned soap and water. Hey, you did it when you were a kid. Call it payback.

Rule 8:
Say farewell to your boat (or other toy) savings.

That money you have worked so hard for and been saving for your dream boat will most likely transition into a college savings fund. Take a breath. It will all be okay.

Look at the bright side: maybe your children will thank you for the college degree by buying you a boat when they have made their millions . . . or maybe they'll thank you by paying for your assisted living costs.

Daddy Data: In case you needed some added motivation, in the United States, the average cost to attend college in 2010–2011 was between $7,605 and $27,293 (per year), not including room and board.[4] That's potentially over $100,000 for a four-year degree! So maybe the boat savings will not be enough, but it is a good start.

Rule 9:
Watch cartoons
with your children.

Remember what it was like to be a kid? Children love cartoons. But your kids love cartoons even more if you watch them with them. Dancing fruit and singing purple monsters may not be your ideal choice of entertainment, but if you were going to spend the time in front of the television anyway, why not spend it with your kids? You'll be amazed at how much fun you can have if you want to.

But be careful: not all cartoons are suitable for children. There are a few popular animated sitcoms that are especially offensive. If you do not monitor what they watch, you may end up having some rather embarrassing conversations.

Daddy Tip: If you cannot live without watching sports or the news, say hello to your new best friend, the DVR or TiVo.

Rule 10:
Sharing is not optional.

Be prepared to share your food, drinks, and treats with your children. When you're eating out, whatever you order will always look better to your children than what they have. It won't be long before you have one or two of your children sitting on your lap, helping themselves to your food. You better start liking mac and cheese, hotdogs, and chicken nuggets, because you'll end up eating their food instead.

Rule 11:
What's yours is theirs.

This rule is closely related to Rule 10, but on a much broader scale. When your children are young, they'll take over your toothbrush and your bed. As they grow older, you'll discover that they have assumed your clothes, your money, and your car. Before you know it, you will have given them your home and will be asking if you can live with them. Think of it as the urban equivalent to the circle of life.

Rule 12:
Develop the ability to block out screaming children.

Warning! You have to hone this skill carefully in order to distinguish between everyday screaming and "Dad, I'm really hurt" screaming. It's a very fine line that you can easily confuse, which can be a problem. For example, ignoring a child who just crashed on his or her bike will get you in trouble with your wife and the child.

Rule 13:
Load at least a dozen kid-friendly games onto your cell phone.

Choose wisely. Having the right games handy could save you from whining or, even worse, tantrums. It's amazing how tossing irritated birds across a screen can calm the most hyper child.

Daddy Tip: If you need some ideas on what games to load onto your phone, go to parenting .com or parents.com, where you will find some great suggestions. Or you could just search through the kid's games categories on your phone's "app" store. I also suggest asking other parents what games their kids like. And since it is for them, you could try asking your own brood what they would like.

Rule 14:
Brush up on your math.

Thought you were done with math when you graduated from college? Think again. Your children still have to go through geometry, algebra, trigonometry, and calculus, which means you do too. And don't forget that there is also English, geography, science, and so much more.

Daddy Tip: If you are struggling with any of these subjects, you may want to check out khanacademy.org, where you will find a library of over 2,700 videos covering everything from arithmetic to physics, finance, and history—a great resource for you and for your children.

Rule 15:
Weekends are for children.

Weekends are no longer for you and your interests, but for kids' soccer games, ballet recitals, Sunday school, and chores. It may take a while to wean yourself from Saturday and Sunday sports, but you can do it. Those of us who have suffered through the same quitting process (and won) salute you and wish you good luck.

Side effects could include a nervous twitch every time you hear game-day music or a racing heart whenever you see your favorite teams logo on a hat or sweatshirt. Other side effects include nausea when you realize you are missing your favorite team's game while you watch your five-year-old in the *Nutcracker*. After a while, these side effects will wane, and you will actually start enjoying the new slate of weekend activities. (Don't give up hope; little boys grow up to be teenage boys who will want to watch and play sports with you.)

Rule 16:
If your kids think it's fun, it should be fun for you.

Yes, this rule can be extremely boring and even painful at first. It will require patience and long-suffering to not only endure but also genuinely enjoy watching Barbie movies, playing hide-and-seek, being the tickle monster, and running through sprinklers . . . or in other words, just being a kid again.

> *"To bring up a child in the way he should go, travel that way yourself once in a while."*
>
> —*Josh Billings*

Rule 17:
Never apply logic to weddings.

The biggest mistake you could possibly make as a father would be to suggest having a barbecue in your backyard as an option for your daughter's wedding reception. I know that this seems like a perfectly acceptable and logical solution. What could be better than food everyone likes? And what could be more convenient than having it in the place your daughter grew up? You could even donate all of the money you saved to the new bride and groom. If you were tracking with my logic, you would be dead wrong! Logical reasoning does not apply to your daughter's (or your wife's) emotional attachments to this special day. I won't even try explaining this one further. Just trust me, and keep your mouth shut.

Daddy Tip: If you want to see a great example of this rule in practice, watch the movie *Father of the Bride*. It may save you a whole lot of heartache and heartburn.

Rule 18:
Stay out of the wedding planning completely.

Rule 17 is so important that it needed a second rule for emphasis and reinforcement. Staying out of the wedding planning completely is really best for your state of mind, your marriage, your relationship, your children, and your health in general. Remember, when it comes to weddings, a father's role is to pay the bills and give the bride away. That is it. The end. No really . . . let it go.

Daddy Tip: There is one more role fathers play in weddings: that of doing as you are told. Just because you are not an active part of the planning committee doesn't mean you will not be given a honey-do list and put to work as the Wedding Gopher (an official title used by wedding planners worldwide that is specifically assigned to fathers).

Rule 19:
Be okay with wearing pink.

If you have girls, you will eventually find yourself decked out in a hot pink tie or polo shirt. It's true. This is an opportunity to show your kids you are comfortable with your masculinity. I also employ another trick. I repeat a line over and over again that I think I got from a movie some time ago: "Pink is this year's black. Pink is this year's black." That seems to calm me down . . . most of the time.

Rule 20:
Learn to love carpools.

J ust because western society has labeled some
women as "soccer moms" doesn't mean you
should label your wife that too. Remember you are
equal partners in this crazy and wonderful thing we
call parenthood. So when you get home at night,
take turns driving the aforementioned minivan (see
Rule 2) to soccer, dance, gymnastics, or baseball
practice. It is also a great time to catch up with your
kids on what is happening in their lives, if you can
hear them over the noise that accompanies a rowdy
bunch of kids in a minivan.

Rule 21:
Showing affection isn't going to hurt you, but withholding your affection will hurt your kids.

Giving lots of hugs and kisses is a requirement, not a request. You may be saying, "Hey, wait a minute. I am a man's man and that's just not what I do. I change my own oil; I own several hunting rifles; I have put a nail through my hand without shedding one tear. I don't hug or kiss." I have news for you, tough guy—it is time to change. Kids need more than a slap on the back to feel validated and loved. While there are more studies on this topic than almost any other, I know you don't need me to list them for you to believe me. You know it's true. By the way, this applies to your boys too.

Daddy Tip: If you want a list of some of those suggested books and websites to help with this and other rules, check out the "Daddy Resources" at the end of the book.

Rule 22:
Start saving now; kids always cost more than you think.

I n Rule 8, we covered the cost to attend college, but it starts a lot earlier with diapers and formula, and progresses to everyday clothing and then to annual dance dresses and sport uniforms. Then come the high-ticket items like orthodontics, prom dresses, and car insurance. If you don't start saving early, I give you two words: second mortgage.

Daddy Data: In 2010, the average total family expenses on a child through age seventeen was $323,380.[4]

Rule 23:
The proper position of the toilet seat is down.

Men and women have been quarrelling over this trivial detail since the invention of the modern toilet. But let's be honest, do you really think we are going to win this argument? Not a chance, my brothers. It's time we swallow our pride and take one extra second to lift or lower the seat and lid whenever we interact with the porcelain throne. (Or you could buy one of those fancy toilet seats that lower the lid themselves.)

What has this got to do with being a good father? By following this one rule, your girls (and especially your wife) will appreciate you more, and your sons will hopefully learn from your example . . . hopefully.

Think of it as helping out the next generation by putting a stop to the "toilet seat controversy."

Rule 24:
Being happy is better than being right.

You have probably heard this advice before, like at your wedding reception, from at least a dozen older men. That's because it's true. Having your wife and kids happy has a direct impact on your happiness. So lose the smug smart-aleck attitude and you'll be much happier, I promise. I unfortunately speak from sad experience. I would have been a lot happier earlier in my fatherhood (and marriage) if I had listened to the men who shared this rule with me at my wedding.

Rule 25:
Become a competent chef.

There will be days when your wife is not home, your mother is intentionally not answering her phone, and the kids are starving. Remember: beef jerky, cold cereal, and ice cream do not a dinner make. For catastrophic times like these, be prepared to put on an apron, take out the pots and pans, and make something fairly healthy and edible for the family. I recommend having five to seven quick and easy "go-to" meals on hand—meals you know your children love and that you are comfortable making. While it may be easier to load the crew into the minivan and get fast food at the closest drive-through, don't do it. Be a good dad by being a health-conscious dad.

Daddy Data: Studies show that childhood obesity has more than tripled in the past thirty years, and the percentage of children aged six to eleven years in the United States who were obese increased from 7 percent in 1980 to nearly 20 percent in 2008. In 2008, more than one third of children and adolescents were overweight or obese.[5] Be a solution, not an accomplice, to this growing problem.

Rule 26:
Replace the remote control with bedtime stories.

While there are some days I wish I could just sit down in my favorite chair, remote in hand, and flip through the channels, I have realized that those days are gone. My wife has also reminded me that I am welcome to relax in front of the television if I want to be a bachelor again. Needless to say, I have chosen to stay married. Plus, it is amazing how quickly your children grow. If you don't put the remote down and pick up a book instead, before you know it they will be too old to read to. And you can never get that time back.

"Any man today who returns from work, sinks into a chair, and calls for his pipe is a man with an appetite for danger."

—Bill Cosby

Rule 27:
Don't take eye-rolling personally.

This innate behavior found in most children usually starts appearing in the preteen years (although it has been known to arrive sooner in some children), lingers for a few annoying years, and typically fizzles out completely by the early twenties. Don't take it personally—it comes with each child.

Daddy Tip: This same strange behavior of rolling one's eyes to the back of one's head does occasionally show up with one's spouse. This is usually a sign that you have really messed up. In this instance, you should take it personally, or else you will be in deep trouble.

Rule 28:
Stress less about the mess.

As we have already addressed in Rule 7, kids are messy—from dirty clothes on the floor, to unwashed dishes in the sink and on the table, to toys underfoot in every room. Kids should come with a warning tag that reads "May cause extreme clutter."

But try not to stress, or be distressed, the next time you trip over a skateboard, or stand on an open stick of lipstick, or find your living room has been transformed into a makeshift fort of pillows and blankets. Instead of yelling, think about how much fun they are having and join them. You can all clean up after the fun is over.

Daddy Tip: Ensure that you have a decent supply of traditional cleaning products on hand since you never know when you are going to need them. There are also some nontraditional cleaning tips you may not have heard of: cornmeal absorbs grease on light colored fabric or upholstery; baby powder sprinkled on a shirt's underarms and collar prevents sweat stains; and car wax can be used to polish faucets, tiles, and doors. For more great ideas on cleaning up messes, check out doityourself.com.

Rule 29:
Take dance lessons.

For starters, take dance lessons so that you can dance with your wife in front of your children. Do it even if you are severely handicapped in this arena and have no rhythm whatsoever. It will teach your children that it's okay to show affection to the ones you love, that you are in love with each other, and that you have a sense of humor.

But the most important reason to take dance lessons is so you can dance with your kids. Whether you are swinging them around or they are trying to stand on your feet while you shimmy around, kids love to dance. So get out your dance shoes and have some fun.

Daddy Tip: By the way, if you do not want to pay for lessons, you can access hundreds of free dance lessons on YouTube, from ballroom dancing to hip hop.

Rule 30:
Always have a backup plan.

Sometimes things will not go according to plan, regardless of how good the plan is. Tires will blow, kids will have blowouts (see Rule 3) and blow-ups, and plans will just go bad. If you don't have a backup plan, life can be stressful. Even with a backup plan, life may still be stressful. While you cannot plan or anticipate every potential mishap, there are some things you can prepare for, like always having enough baby wipes and diapers on hand or keeping enough cash in your wallet for the unexpected snafus.

For the unfortunate events that completely surprise you, you may have to just suck it up and deal with it.

PART 2:

What Dads Should Say

PART 2:

What Dads Should Say

Often what we mean to say and what is actually communicated are two very different things. Luckily, this is an ailment not only suffered by dads alone, but anyone who is encumbered by using the English language.

George Carlin put it best when he asked, "Why do we park in the driveway and drive on the parkway? Or why do we recite at a play and play at a recital? Ship by truck and send cargo by ship? Have noses that run and feet that smell?"[6]

Not only are we burdened with the challenge of using the English language correctly, but think about how much more difficult it is to communicate when you also add in the complexities of emotions and personality traits.

So the next time you are at a loss for what to say, just pull out *Dad Rules* and scan this section. I hope there is at least one rule that covers the issue you are dealing with. If not, return to Rule 31 and start again.

Rule 31:
Learn when to say nothing at all.

Whenever you find yourself completely perplexed during a parent-child dialogue, stop thinking about what you are going to say next and listen. Try to really understand what your child is saying, and then listen some more just to make sure.

Saying nothing is often the best solution, especially when it is an emotionally charged conversation that you cannot rationally explain (you can expect a lot of these during the teen years). In these instances, saying anything would only make matters worse, so use your communication appendages proportionately . . . two ears first, one mouth last (if at all).

This rule is so important that Stephen R. Covey, author of *The 7 Habits of Highly Effective People*, even dedicated one of his seven habits to it: "Seek first to understand and then to be understood."[7]

"You say it best when you say nothing at all."

—*Alison Krauss*

Rule 32:
If you don't know, then say, "I don't know."

Kids are smart enough to see through the fluff, especially in their teenage years, so be honest with them. Admitting you are not the all-knowing father figure will get you major points with your children (unless you are just saying it to just brush them off). Nothing is more annoying than a know-it-all, especially if that person happens to be your dad. However, make sure you follow up your genuine admission of knowledge deficit with the offer to help them discover the answer.

Rule 33:
When you mess up, say "I'm sorry."

T his is another rule that will endear your children to you. You are not perfect. You make mistakes like everybody else. You know it, and they know it—so why not teach your children a valuable lesson by sincerely saying you are sorry?

"Apology is a lovely perfume; it can transform the clumsiest moment into a gracious gift."

—*Margaret Lee Runbeck*

Rule 34:
When your child is right, say so.

Regardless of how difficult it may be to take advice and correction from your children, sometimes it is the right thing to do. However, in order for this rule to work properly, you first have to give them permission to help you be a better dad. Ask them to tell you when you are not treating them like you should or when you stand in need of correction. Second, have the courage to listen to their comments and suggestions without being defensive. Children can be brutally honest, but sometimes that is exactly what we need to hear. Last, change your behavior. (And you thought your mother-in-law was the only one telling you what you can do to improve.)

Rule 35:
Never say, "Because I said so; that's why."

Think about how much this same statement bugged you when you were a kid. It's a cop-out and it communicates that you don't want your children to think for themselves. If you really don't want to debate or discuss something with your children, tell them that instead. That way you at least show them respect and you are not being a total jerk.

Rule 36:
Live with gratitude in your heart and on your tongue.

Growing up poor in South Africa helped me appreciate the little things in life. As a father, you have the opportunity and responsibility to help your children create an attitude of gratitude. But to do this effectively, you must carry that same attitude within yourself. This will teach your kids valuable lessons about blessings, abundance, and how not to feel like they are entitled to material possessions.

"Gratitude is the sign of noble souls."

—*Aesop*

Rule 37:
Don't "@#$%&"

Be creative enough to never curse. Everyone has those moments in life when a thumb is smashed with a hammer, or a hand is slammed in the car door, and the only thing that seems to help alleviate the pain is to shout something. Well, if you have to shout, yell something other than a vulgar curse word. Be respectful of those around you, especially your children. Be appropriately creative. I actually made up a word that has worked well for me for over twenty years: "apokadiggie." That's right, I yell "apokadiggie!" whenever I stub my toe. That's my word; make up your own.

Rule 38:
Say "I love you" often.

Y our children cannot read your mind, just as you cannot read theirs. And don't assume they know you love them. They need to hear their father say three of the most precious words in any language, "I love you." And I am not talking about doing it once a year on their birthday. That doesn't count. You need to tell them often. Actually, put down this book and go tell them right now. (Text or call them if they are not physically around.) And please don't stop following this rule even after they have left home.

A bell is no bell 'til you ring it,
A song is no song 'til you sing it,
And love in your heart
Wasn't put there to stay —
Love isn't love
'Til you give it away.

—*Oscar Hammerstein, Sound of Music,*
"You Are Sixteen (Reprise)"

Rule 39:
Let your children hear you tell your wife you love her.

I know all this talk of "love" may be making some of you men a little uncomfortable, but bear with me; I am almost through.

Not only do your children need to hear those words from you to them, they also need to hear you tell their mother. I always thought I was pretty good with this rule, until my dear wife taught me a precious lesson. She said, "Treion, thank you for telling me you love me, but what I really want to hear is why you love me."

Now, take note. Whatever you do, don't tell her—especially in front of the kids—that you love her because she is beautiful. I have also made this mistake. She doesn't want your kids to think that beauty is the only definition of love or that appearances are all that matter. Yes, it is acceptable to say you love her for her beauty, as long as you also mention other attributes and qualities you love about her too.

I know I have taken three simple words and complicated it with a list of criteria and steps, but I'm just trying to share what I have learned the hard way.

Rule 40:
Always praise.

Children need praise. They need encouragement. They need to feel validated, and they need to hear you publicly praise them. These priceless little gems are ours to mold, especially in their early formative and impressionable years. Be gentle and loving with how you mold these precious and tender spirits. Look for opportunities to praise them. Even commenting on a seemingly small and unimportant thing you saw your child do or say goes a long way to build their self-esteem.

> *"Affirming words from moms and dads are like light switches. Speak a word of affirmation at the right moment in a child's life and it's like lighting up a whole roomful of possibilities."*
>
> —Gary Smalley

Rule 41:
Never demean.

Thumper, the little rabbit in the classic children's movie *Bambi*, gives one of the wisest and most profound statements ever uttered, "If you can't say something nice, don't say nothing at all." Enough said.

Rule 42:
Be your singing
child's biggest fan.

A singing child is a happy child. While you may get sick of hearing the same song over and over again and be tempted to ask your kid to be quiet, don't! Allow them to express themselves and their joy through song. Plus, it makes other people around them happy too. Every time I have been in a grocery store with one of my singing sunshines, I have watched all the people we come into earshot of do the same thing: smile. It's contagious. You cannot help yourself. The sound of a young child singing is truly one of the sweetest sounds there is.

Daddy Tip: Encourage your singing phenom by buying (or downloading) some of the fun compilation CDs and mp3s now available. You can choose from "30 Toddler Songs," "Disney Princesses Songs," "Sesame Street Favorites"— the list goes on and on and on . . . just like the songs they tend to sing.

Rule 43:
Use the "magic words" yourself.

In Rule 36, we introduced the importance of saying one of these magic phrases, "thank you." There are more. But beware: hypocrisy is an ugly friend to have and a very bad example to your children. So make new friends. If you have forgotten to use the magic words, become reacquainted. I promise it will be a prosperous reuniting. In case you have forgotten, the magic words are "please," "thank you," and "you're welcome."

"If there is anything we wish to change in the child, we should first examine it and see whether it is not something that could better be changed in ourselves."

—Carl Jung

Rule 44:
The answer to, "Dad, can I show you something?" is always, "Yes!"

I f you take the time to watch your children skip, do endless jumps, ride without hands, and other kid stuff when they are young, they will more likely allow you to be involved in their lives when they are older. I think that's a fair trade, don't you?

> *"A really great man never puts away the simplicity of a child."*
>
> —*Chinese proverb*

Rule 45:
If you feel the urge to lecture, stop and think about it first.

R emember Rule 31? Sometimes it's best to not say anything, especially if what you wanted to say can be classified as a "lecture." If you are in the heat of a discussion and you feel a "finger wagging, I-know-what's-best" discourse coming on, stop and think about it first. Ask yourself if your condescending tone and macho message will help the situation or make it worse. In most cases, you will find that it will not help, so just don't go there.

"Keep your words soft and tender because tomorrow you may have to eat them."

—*Author Unknown*

Rule 46:
Consult your wife
on what to say.

One example of this rule would be to talk to her before saying anything negative about an item of clothing your daughter is wearing. Just trust me on this one. If you are thinking of saying, "you are not leaving my house wearing that," then hold your tongue and first talk to your wife about it. And if your assessment of the outfit was correct, then let her break the news in a kinder, gentler way. There are just some things our wives are much better at doing. This is one of those things.

Rule 47:
Create "pet names" for your children.

Some older kids may not like to be called cutie pie, monkey, pumpkin, junior, bell, or chip, but they love it when they are young. And some even choose to be called by that nickname throughout their lives.

I have taken this rule one step further by actually having a specific song for each kid, some made-up and some well-known ditties. While I do not have a great voice, I sure sing these songs to my kids with gusto and loads of animation.

This seemingly crazy behavior communicates that you care enough for them to show affection, especially if it is potentially embarrassing. Like singing, "Sugar pie honey bunch, you know I love you" at the top of your lungs while mixing in some disco moves. You know you have succeeded if your performance elicits smiles, laughs, and even some eye-rolling.

Rule 48:
Remember to laugh at yourself.

Don't take yourself or life's little irritants so seriously. Spilling your favorite beverage all over the kitchen floor is not the worst thing that can happen. Getting mad over it, however, is.

Some things are funny, even if it involves you taking a tumble. You can choose to make a big deal out of it and make everyone around you uncomfortable, or you can choose to laugh at yourself and enjoy life a lot more.

"For every minute you are angry, you lose sixty seconds of happiness."

—*Anonymous*

Rule 49:
Don't say anything you wouldn't want your grandmother to hear.

Or you wouldn't want to see on YouTube, on Facebook, or in the paper. Whenever you are in doubt about what to say, remember this rule. It should be easy enough if you just imagine that your grandmother (or mother) is a witness to the conversation. If you would not say it in her presence, don't say it.

When I find myself engaged in a heated dialogue with one of my children, I picture my grandmother with her hands on hips, staring at with me with that "what did you just say?" expression on her face.

Just reading the preceding sentence probably caused some of you discomfort as you remembered your own grandmother saying something similar to you. Applying this one rule will usually save you a lot of heartburn and stress.

PART 3:

What Dads Should Do

What Dads Should Do

Becoming a dad can be traumatic. One minute it's just you and your wife, and the next minute there is a whole other person you're responsible for. Add in the shocking experience of witnessing childbirth, and it's no wonder new fathers always look so overwhelmed. No warning, just *bam!* You are a daddy now.

Then again, being a dad can also be traumatic. There are many moments in life that we fathers share—like when your daughter rolls her eyes and storms out of the room, or when your son pees in the neighbor's rose garden. You know, those times when you think, "What the apokadiggie do I do now?"

This section of the book makes fatherhood a little less traumatic by helping you know what to do in those unforeseen moments.

Rule 50:
Show your children you love them.

While it is absolutely essential to say the three words (see Rule 38), there are also other ways of saying "I love you," without actually saying it. Some other three-word combinations that also say "I love you" are:

- Hide and seek
- Date with daddy
- Hugs and kisses
- Tickle monster wrestling
- Throw and catch
- Create your own

Daddy Data: "Decades of research reveal ten essential parenting skill sets. . . . Giving love and affection tops the list."[8]

Rule 51:
Be a real man.

Real men provide, support, love, and cry. They praise, comfort, sacrifice, are patient, and stand for something. Above all, real men revere womanhood and treat women with respect.

A real man is far from what the entertainment world claims a real man is. If you are looking to the artificial world of movies and television for the characteristics of a good dad, you will be generally disappointed. While there may be a few exceptions, most father figures in showbiz are not a great representation of what dads should do or say. (Go back to Rule 4 to read from whom you should be seeking advice.)

Rule 52:
Be proud of your Daddy status.

Being a dad is an awesome privilege. After all, you are the king of your kingdom, the captain of your team, the chief mucky-muck . . . when your wife allows you to be, that is. Be proud of your status.

I love going into an office and finding photos of that man's children on his desk and stick figure drawings on his walls. You can tell that these are men who are proud to be fathers. They are the type of guys who wear the "World's Greatest Dad" T-shirt until it is threadbare, because it was a gift from their kids, and who have hundreds of family pictures on their phones that they are willing to share with complete strangers. Tough, hard-hat wearing men, men who melt when their little baby girl cups their hardened chin in her tiny hands—these are the real men we spoke of in the previous rule.

This rule is your bold declaration to the world that you are a dad and proud of it. So whenever you are struggling with any of the other rules, remember to come back to this one, recommit yourself, and then get back to work.

Rule 53:
If the technology doesn't include your kids, put it away.

This rule has been around for a long time. Despite the longevity of this principle, we are sometimes still very bad about bringing work home. We will often give more attention to a computer screen, newspaper, or touch screen than we do to our kids. When you get home, the only thing you should turn on is Daddy mode. You already spend more time at work than you do awake at home. Besides being mentally and physically present for them, it also teaches your kids to put away their own electronics, a practice you will be grateful for when they are texting teenagers.

Daddy Data (in case you needed a reason to turn off the technology): The average teenager sends and receives 3,339 text messages per month.[9] Since almost all Americans (85 percent) now own a cell phone,[10] this number will continue to grow.

Rule 54:
Give up a GNO (guys' night out) for a date night with your girls.

Date nights are a must if you want to have a good relationship with your daughters. While you may have to sacrifice something you like doing, you will end up doing something you love, with someone you love. For more on this principle, I recommend going back to Rule 1. It is, after all, a very good place to start.

Rule 55:
Raise children,
not clones of you.

This may be a hard rule to follow, because we are all very good at knowing what we want, how we think, and what we are good at. It is human nature to default to our own frame of reference and experiences. But we need to remember that each child is unique. We must not only accept their different skills and talents but also embrace them. And then take it one step further and encourage them to follow their hearts, passions, and interests.

This rule will help you when your son chooses dance over sports or accounting over law school. His choices may not be what you had hoped, but it is his choice after all, and he is not a miniature version of you.

Rule 56:
Discipline, but do it with love.

Common sense and hundreds of studies tell us we need to discipline our children. The challenge is how to do it the right way. While there are many books that go into much more detail on the topic, I always turn to the master teacher, Jesus Christ, for the answer. Not only did he exemplify this principle throughout his life, but he also taught it to his disciples. We learn from one of those disciples, John, that "There is no fear in love; but perfect love casteth out fear" (1 John 4:18). So when you do discipline, if you do it with love, you will have a much better chance of getting it right. (For more on disciplining your children, refer to the daddy resources at the end of the book.)

> *"And, ye fathers, provoke not your children to wrath: but bring them up in the nurture and admonition of the Lord."*
>
> —*Ephesians 6:4*

Rule 57:
Be a dad first and a friend second.

As a father, you sometimes have to be "the enforcer." If you are a friend first, you may be reluctant to discipline and lay down the law, because that is not what friends do. But that is what dads have to do, so be wise in where you choose to draw the line.

> *"The thing that impresses me most about America is the way parents obey their children."*
>
> —*Edward, Duke of Windsor, Look,*
> *5 March 1957*

Rule 58:
Play video games with your children.

F irst, ensure that you have clear rules on the amount of playing time and on the type of games that are allowed (see Rule 63). Then make it a habit to occasionally play with your children. But be prepared for them to kick your behind, because your old-timer Atari skills will not help you in this new era of gaming. But whether you win or lose, what a great way to spend one-on-one time with your kids. It also allows you to see the type of games they are playing; there are some violent and sexually explicit games you want to block from your home and your child's life.

Daddy Data: Watch for signs of gaming addiction in your children, and beware of addiction yourself. Yes, this is a real addiction. Some dads spend days on end playing various types of online games, neglecting their duties as father. If you or your child suffers from gaming addiction, seek help. For starters, go to the several online resources, like On-Line Gamers Anonymous.[11]

Rule 59:
Wherever you go, take one of your children with you.

Teaching moments are best when they are spontaneously shared in the seams of the day. Look for these moments, make these moments, and cherish these moments. A trip to the grocery store or to get a haircut is a great opportunity to catch up and spend quality time with a child.

I was recently traveling for work when I ran into a high-powered attorney friend who was traveling to meet with a client. He had his eleven-year-old daughter with him. What a great example of this rule in action.

Rule 60:
Shoot more videos and take more photos.

Trust me on this one; you always wish you had more videos and photos. With the way digital technology has evolved, keeping this rule should be easy. Most of us have a decent camera on our phones that we can pull out in a moments notice. Use it more often; you will not be sorry.

Daddy Tip: Take all of your old printed photos and negatives to be digitized. It doesn't cost a lot of money and is a great way to digitally store and protect them. Then buy an external hard drive for each of your children, where you store their photos and videos.

Rule 61:
Be social media smart.

I am not suggesting you have to be online all day reading people's status updates, but you should at least be savvy enough to be friends with your kids on Facebook and other social media sites. (According to a recent 2010 survey, more than nine in ten teens [93 percent] who use social media have a Facebook account.) [12]

This is how they are choosing to communicate with their friends, so think of it as a great way to stay in touch with your kids and still be their guardian and protector.

Daddy Data: According to teens, parents who use social media are more likely to talk with them about what kinds of things should and should not be shared online or on a cell phone. Teens report that parents who are friends with their teens on social media are more likely to have these conversations than parents who have not "friended" their child (92 percent vs. 79 percent).[12]

Rule 62:
Protect your kids from harmful online influences.

I f you are like me, you probably walk through your house each night to make sure that all the doors and windows are locked, because you want to protect your family from all potential danger.

If you place so much effort and attention to protecting your family from physical danger, why wouldn't you also protect them from online predators and the destructive influence of pornography? While the Internet has become a great source of knowledge, it's also filled with filth that innocent fingers can easily stumble upon. This "window" also needs to be carefully monitored. Load robust filters [13] and protections on all your computers, so you don't unintentionally invite unwelcome visitors into your home. Another good practice is to place computers in areas of the home where the screen is visible to everyone.

Daddy Data: Unfortunately, there are far too many scary statistics regarding this rule. Here are just two: 60 percent of all website visits are sexual in nature,[14] and 79 percent of unwanted exposure to pornography occurs in the home. [15]

Rule 63:
Be clear on their rules.

Establish clear rules and expectations with your kids around television watching, computer and cell phone use, dating, dinnertime, homework, sleepovers, family time, friends, video games, movies, and chores. Rules are a great way of providing necessary boundaries and guidelines. It provides a safety net for children and peace of mind for dads.

Daddy Tip: Consider creating a "Wordle" (wordle.net) or word cloud made up of the words found in your family's rules that you can frame and hang up in your home.

Rule 64:
Stay involved in your children's lives.

Make sure you know who your kids friends are and what activities they are participating in. You can learn about this information first-hand by volunteering at their school, being their soccer coach, or taking karate with them. You should also try to meet all of your kids' friends and dates. This does not mean that you should try and emulate the old movie stereotype of the father cleaning his shotgun while talking to the boyfriend. That is just plain scary. You can still be pleasant to friends and dates without being weird and obnoxious (see the next rule). Plus, being nice will make them want to include you in their life more.

Rule 65:
Be friendly to your children's friends

It is sometimes hard enough to practice patience with your own offspring, not to mention the dozen additional neighborhood kids who seem to always be at your home eating your food and teaching your kids bad jokes. But aren't you glad they are hanging out at your home where you can keep a close eye on what they are doing? Be nice to your kid's friends, so they want to gather in your home, instead of somewhere else . . . where you may not know what activities are permitted.

Rule 66:
Set family time aside, or you'll lose it.

Life can get busy, and the hours in our days will fill up with meaningless busy work if we are not careful. So ensure that you block out time for your kids. Have a scheduled routine that is sacred and cannot be replaced by other priorities, no matter how important.

Almost all human beings, including kids, like routine. We find comfort in routine. Knowing what to expect and having consistency in a sometimes hectic schedule is a wonderful reprieve.

Rule 67:
Have frequent one-on-one talks with each child.

Make this rule part of Rule 66 and block out specific time to informally talk to your children. It doesn't take long to sit down with one child at a time and ask them about their friends, how they are doing in school, what concerns or challenges they are facing, and what their hopes are for next week and for the future. But it does provide a safe environment for them to open up if they need to, and it communicates that you care enough about them to ask about their lives. For this rule to be effective, you need to remember once again to practice Rule 31 and just listen.

Rule 68:
Establish a healthy dose of family traditions.

Traditions bind families and create lasting memories. If your wife isn't already on top of this rule (which she probably is), take charge yourself. Some fathers I spoke to celebrate Christmas in July, go caroling in December, create an annual family YouTube video, host a Halloween party, sing karaoke, plan a family sleepover at a local hotel, engage in full-scale Nerf-gun wars, and participate in Thanksgiving bingo. But the best traditions are the ones that involve serving others, like Secret Santa or Sub for Santa.

There are so many cool traditions just waiting to be enjoyed. Which ones will you start doing? (Make sure you don't forget to consult your wife and children on this rule since it involves them as well.)

Daddy Tip: One family tradition idea is to start a family website. There are many free sites that make it easy for you to share blogs, pictures, and videos, such as familydetails.com, shutterfly.com, easysite.com, and, of course, Facebook.

Rule 69:
Celebrate your children.

Make a big deal out of the big and the small successes. Taking your kid to Europe as a reward for graduating high school with honors is a good practice. Taking your kids to dinner for doing their chores for the month is even better, because you can enjoy more of these small celebrations throughout the years.

Look for reasons to celebrate often. Make life fun for your children and for you. It also communicates that you appreciate the little things as much as the big things they do.

"All children behave as well as they are treated"

—Anonymous

Rule 70:
Make your kids work for their rewards.

I call this is the "anti-entitlement" rule. In a world of excess and limitless material possessions, our children are sometimes victims of overindulgence and feelings of entitlement. "I want" and "I get" are often synonymous. They ask, and we give.

Beware! This seemingly innocent practice just feeds into an already growing culture of entitlement. If you love your children, make them work for their rewards. They will learn to associate work with positive rewards, which will prepare them for a life that requires them to work.

Rule 71:
If you want to teach the value of hard work, work hard.

The previous rule works even better if you also follow it up with this rule. Telling is never as effective as showing. A child who sees his father washing the dishes is more likely to clean the kitchen. A child who sees her father painting a ceiling is more likely to pick up a brush and paint the walls. This principle is not rocket science and has been around a lot longer than any of us. So just trust this old adage and get to work.

Daddy Data: According to the United States Bureau of Labor Statistics, on an average day, 20 percent of men did housework (such as cleaning or doing laundry) compared with 49 percent of women.[16] Come on, gentlemen; let's put this rule into play and help our wives out in the process.

Rule 72:
Teach the basics early.

There are some basic skills that every functional human being, including your children, should know how to do—skills like how to keep a budget, boil water, iron a shirt, do laundry, start a dishwasher, work a vacuum, jump a dead car battery, change a tire, make a bed, polish shoes, change a light bulb, or start a lawn mower.

Don't assume your kids will just learn how to do these things by osmosis. That's why they have parents. It is amazing how many kids don't know how to perform some of these basic life skills when they first leave home for college or marriage. This can really be embarrassing. Imagine your college-aged son not being able to make up a box of mac and cheese or wash his clothes. Or your newly married daughter not knowing how to vacuum her new apartment. Come on, dads; give them a hand while you still can. I promise you they will be grateful you took the time to teach them these basic skills.

Rule 73:
Teach them everything you know, and then some.

Along with Rule 72, if you follow this rule, it means you are spending the right amount of time with your kids.

You may be surprised to find out how much you know if you took a moment to write everything down. Go ahead; give it a try. Just write down everything you can think of, and don't minimize the small things. Sometimes those are the things that fascinate your children the most. Write down everything from changing a tire to changing the oil, from flying a kite to folding a paper airplane, from how to shave to how to make an ice cave, from tying a tie to tying a fly, from painting a wall to painting a canvas, from shooting a rifle to shooting a camera, from baking a cake to grilling a steak. The possibilities for fun are endless.

Daddy Tip: Repeat the exercise, but this time sit down with your children and write down everything you don't know but would like to learn. As you brainstorm together, keep long- and short-term learning goals in mind.

Rule 74:
Keep learning, and share what you learn with your children.

Even though you may have already graduated from college, remain a student. Always be engaged in learning something new, whether formal or informal. You can join a book club, teach yourself how to assemble a car engine, or learn how to speak a different language.

But here is the key to this rule: share what you are learning with your kids, or even better, involve them in what you learning. For example, you can give them a copy of the book you are reading, or get them under the hood of a car with you, or teach them how to greet someone in a new language. Only once you are able to transfer what you learn to someone else is learning fully accomplished.

"Tell me, I'll forget; show me and I may remember; involve me and I'll understand"

—*Chinese proverb*

Rule 75:
See through their eyes.

Try looking at the world through your children's eyes.

Even seemingly small events in a child's life can take on new meaning if you try to experience them through the eyes of your child who is discovering them for the first time.

Like the time my one-year-old daughter first discovered wind. She was intently focused on something in the nearby trees. My more mature eyes could not make out what she was looking at. She would not avert her attention anywhere else. Then I finally saw what she was seeing. She was watching the breeze as it gently caressed the leaves to and fro. This was the first time she had experienced wind, and I was privileged to enjoy that moment with her.

While the magnitude of these moments varies and decreases over time, there are still plenty of them to be enjoyed. Like a baby's first words, splashing in a tub, being potty trained, riding a bike, flying a kite, learning to read, learning to swim, passing trigonometry, driving a car, falling in love, going to prom, and so on.

All of these moments and a hundred more are

new and exciting treasures waiting to be discovered and shared. You can embrace the adventure and get lost in their exciting world, or let it pass you by. Remember Rule 1—the choice is yours.

Rule 76:
Be a facilitator of fun.

This rule works in tandem with the previous rule. Not only should you try to see the world through the eyes of your children, but you should also seek opportunities to facilitate new and wonderful experiences. Like giving them the window seat in the airplane, putting them on your shoulder during Disneyland's magical parade, or placing a paintbrush in their hand and a large piece of paper in front of them.

Think of yourself as the facilitator of fun or the coordinator of cool. It's amazing where a little imagination can take you and your kids.

"The essence of childhood, of course, is play, which my friends and I did endlessly on streets that we reluctantly shared with traffic."

—Bill Cosby

Rule 77:
Be more mature than your children.

Sulking, pouting, tantrums, eye-rolling, feeling sorry for yourself, and relentless teasing are examples of some unacceptable fatherly behavior. You had your turn when you were young; it is now your turn to be a grown-up.

Daddy Tip: There are exceptions to this rule. Sometimes you need to be as enthusiastic, as carefree, as energetic, as uninhibited, as honest, and as goofy as your children. Because sometimes it is not only acceptable but encouraged to be a kid again (see Rule 76).

Rule 78:
Control your temper.

While a temper is an easy thing to lose, it is unfortunately also easily found again. Blowing up is never a productive alternative to parenting. Yes, it may get your kids to change behavior in that moment, but that's because they are motivated by fear. You never want your children to fear you; you want them to love and respect you. If you struggle with impatience and a short fuse, you may want to spend a lot more time researching and working on this rule. See some of the recommended resources at the end of this book.

> *"Fathers, provoke not your children to anger, lest they be discouraged."*
>
> —*Colossians 3:8*

Rule 79:
Take care of yourself.

I know many of the rules have advocated selfless-
ness and dedication to your children, but if you
are not healthy enough to be around, then you will
not be able to follow all those other rules anyway.

So take care of yourself physically, emotionally, socially, and spiritually. You may need to be
creative with when you make time for yourself,
but it is essential that you do so. For example,
I choose to exercise before the kids get up in the
morning. I also plan a few hours here and there
to do something I like to do, like watch a football game, go out with some friends, or just watch
a movie. No matter what you choose to do with
your time, make sure you schedule some "me"
time or you will burn out.

Daddy Tip: It is essential to always involve your
wife in the planning of those times, so that you can
first get her approval and so that she is aware of
when you will be unavailable.

Rule 80:
If you are not the perfect dad yet, keep at it.

And welcome to the club. While there may be some that are pretty darn close to being perfect, most of us have to show up for the job every day (see Rule 1) and keep on improving.

In the words of country music group Rascal Flatts, "It's a long, slow, beautiful dance, my friend."

So just keep at it. Then one day when you're the one with toxic diapers and your son or daughter is changing you, you will appreciate all the time you spent working on these rules.

Rule 81:
Share with other dads what you have learned.

In Rule 4 you were encouraged to ask other dads for advice, and in this rule you are encouraged to return the favor and look for opportunities to share what you have learned with other dads. Save them from as much heartburn as possible by offering your words of wisdom, especially the rules you learned the hard way.

Another place you can share what you have learned is at Trieon.com or at Dad Rules on Facebook. I would love to learn how you have applied the rules in your life, what new rules you have discovered, and anything else you would like to share with me and other dads.

And please—enjoy the journey. Being a dad is one crazy but beautiful adventure!

Daddy Resources

RECOMMENDED BOOKS:

Foster Cline and Jim Fay, *Parenting With Love and Logic* (Colorado Springs: Pinon Press, 1990).

Laura M. Brotherson, *And They Were Not Ashamed* (Boise: Inspire Books, 2004).

Richard M. Eyre and Linda Eyre, *The Entitlement Trap: How to Rescue Your Child with a New Family System of Choosing, Earning, and Ownership* (New York: Avery, 2011).

Alice Miller, *The Drama of the Gifted Child* (New York: Basic Books, 1981).

Adele Faber and Elaine Mazlish, *How to Talk So Kids Will Listen and Listen So Kids Will Talk* (New York: HarperCollins, 1980).

John W. James and Russell Friedman, *When Children Grieve* (New York: HarperCollins, 2001).

Ruth Reardon, *Listen to My Feelings* (C.R. Gibson, 1992).

John C. Friel, PhD, and Linda D. Friel, MA, *The 7 Worst Things Good Parents Do* (Deerfield Beach: Health Communications, 1999).

Deborah Tannen, *You're Wearing That?* (New York: Random House, 2006).

Anthony E. Wolf and Suzanne Franks, *Get Out of My Life* (London: Profile Books, 1991).

Everett De Morier, *Crib Notes for the First Year of Fatherhood: A Survival Guide for New Fathers* (Minneapolis: Fairview Press, 1998).

Stephen R. Covey, *The 7 Habits of Highly Effective People* (New York: Free Press, 1989).

Sean Covey, *The 7 Habits of Highly Effective Teens* (New York: Free Press, 1998).

RECOMMENDED WEBSITES:

AllProDad.com

BabyCenter.com

ChildUp.com

DoItYourself.com

Enough.org *(Making the internet safer for children and families)*

EasySite.com

FamilyDetails.com

Family.go.com *(Disney's Family Fun magazine)*

FreeTipsForParents.com

http://jfi.sagepub.com *(Journal of Family Issues)*

KhanAcademy.org

Parents.com

Parenting.com

Shutterfly.com

ValuesParenting.com

Wordle.net

Citations

1. Gwen Dewar, PhD, "Newborn Sleep Patterns: A Survival Guide for the Science-Minded Parent," *Parenting Science* http://www.parentingscience.com/newborn-sleep.html.

2. Based on an average of eight changes per day over two years ($8 \times 365 \times 2 = 5,840$).

3. Estimate based on the cost of a diaper being between 23 and 28 cents.

4. United States Department of Agriculture: Center for Nutrition Policy and Promotion, "Miscellaneous Publication 1528–2010," *Expenditures on Children by Families.* http://www.cnpp.usda.gov/ExpendituresonChildrenbyFamilies.htm.

5. Cynthia L. Ogden et al., "Prevalence of High Body Mass Index in US Children and Adolescents, 2007–2008," *Journal of*

the *American Medical Association* 303, no. 3 (2010); Nancy F. Krebs et al., "Assessment of Child and Adolescent Overweight and Obesity," *Pediatrics* 120, supplement 4 (2007).

6. George Carlin, *Brain Droppings* (New York: Hyperion, 2006).

7. Stephen R. Covey, *The 7 Habits of Highly Effective People* (New York: Free Press, 1989), 5.

8. Robert Epstein, "What Makes a Good Parent?" *Scientific American Mind,* November/December 2010, 48.

9. The Nielsen Company, "U.S. Teen Mobile Report: Calling Yesterday, Texting Today, Using Apps Tomorrow," *NielsenWire* (blog), October 14, 2010, blog.nielsen.com/nielsenwire/online_mobile/u-s-teen-mobile-calling-yesterday-texting-today-using-apps-tomorrow.

10. *Pew Research Center's Internet & American Life Project*, http://pewresearch.org/pubs/1484/social-media-mobile-internet-use-teens-millennials-fewer-blog, November 2011.

11. *On-Line Gamers Anonymous*, http://www.olganon.org.

12. *Pew Research Center,* "Internet & American Life Teen-Parent Survey," 2011. http://www.pewinternet.org/Infographics/2011/Teens

-Kindness-and-Cruelty-on-Social-Network
-Sites.aspx

13. *TopTenREVIEWS*, "Internet Filter Software Review," http://internet-filter-review.topten reviews.com.

14. MSNBC/Stanford/Duquesne Study, *Washington Times*, January 26, 2000, as quoted in EnoughIsEnough, http://www.enough.org/ inside.php?tag=stat%20archives.

15. National Center for Missing & Exploited Children, "Online Victimization of Youth: Five Years Later," news release, August 9, 2006, http://www.internetsafety101.org/ Pornographystatistics.htm.

16. Bureau of Labor Statistics, American Time Use Survey Summary, June 22, 2011, http:// www.bls.gov/news.release/atus.nr0.htm.

Special Thanks To...

My seven dads—Uncle Henry and Uncle Justice, Jeffery Swartz Sr., Rick Beeton, Kenneth Armstrong, Brad Stone, and Boyd Mordue. Thanks for being there when I needed a father to look up to.

My friends and support crew—Spencer Mordue, Steve Mordue, Barb Mordue, the rest of the Mordue crew, Penny Stone and the rest of the Stone clan, Sam Bracken, Matt Murdoch, Ruth Barker, Jackie Campbell, Annie Oswald. You have been an inspiration and support for me on this journey through fatherhood. Thanks.

My wife, Soni, for always motivating me to be better and putting up with my many "shortcomings." You are my love, my everything.

And my darling children—Chloe, Layla, Gemma, Ruby, and TJ, for making life so much fun and for being patient with their "work in progress" father. Love you monkeys with all my heart.

About the Author

Treion Muller is a diverse South-African American with a made-up French name who was fortunate to have not one, but seven "surrogate" dads. After his biological dad left when he was young, these seven father figures came into his life at different times and stages and guided him through his youth, teenage years, and into fatherhood.

111

Treion also draws inspiration from his experiences as a professional dancer, medic in the South African Army, missionary, university student body president, university mascot (the Thunderbird), foster parent, and professional speaker.

He is the proud father of five delightful—but not perfect—children, and husband to one amazing wife. The "Muller Mob" now lives on the foothills of the Wasatch Mountains in northern Utah.

When Treion is not driving the car pool in his minivan or whipping up some healthy concoction in his kitchen, you can find him at FranklinCovey working as Chief eLearning Architect, where he co-authored *The Learning Explosion: 9 Rules to Ignite Your Virtual Classroom* and *The Webinar Manifesto.*

Stay in touch with Treion:

Website: Treion.com

Facebook: Dad Rules

Twitter: @Treeon

LinkedIn: linkedin.com/in/treionmuller

0 26575 10315 1